Web3 and Decentralization

Examine How Blockchain Technology and Decentralized Applications Could Upend Conventional Industries

Taylor Royce

Copyright © 2024 Taylor Royce

All rights reserved.

DEDICATION

To all the visionaries and trailblazers shaping the technological landscape of the future, whose unwavering innovation and creative spirit enable the seemingly unachievable.

To those who are dedicated to pushing the limits of technology and who have the audacity to envision a decentralized future.

And to all of my readers who are interested in learning about and embracing Web3 and blockchain technology, may this book encourage and enable you to join me on this life-changing adventure.

CONTENTS

ACKNOWLEDGMENTS 1

Disclaimer 3

CHAPTER 1 1

Overview of Decentralization and Web3 1

    1.1 What is Web3? 1

    1.2 Essential Decentralization Concepts 2

    1.3 The Web's Development: From Web1 to Web3 3

    1.4 The Significance of Decentralization 5

CHAPTER 2 8

Blockchain Technology Unveiled 8

    2.1 Describe Blockchain. Knowing How to Use the Distributed Ledger System 8

    2.2 The Three Fundamental Ideas of Blockchain: Consensus, Transparency, and Immutability 10

    2.3 Distinct Blockchain Types: Permissioned, Private, and Public 12

    2.4 Blockchain Technology's Potential Is Not Limited to Cryptocurrencies 14

CHAPTER 3 19

Explaining Decentralized Apps (dApps) in Simple Terms 19

    3.1 Describe dApps. Blockchain-Based Applications 19

    3.2 Trustless, Permissionless, and Censorship-Resistant dApp Features. 21

    3.3 Popular dApp Examples in Various Industries 22

3.4 Developing and Implementing dApps: Resources and Tools........ 25

CHAPTER 4...29

Web3 and Finance's Future (DeFi)..29

4.1 Decentralized Finance (DeFi): A Financial Services Paradigm Transformation...29

4.2 Revolutionizing Conventional Finance: Financing, Debt, and Exchange in DeFi..30

4.3 DEXs (Decentralized Exchanges): Enabling Users and Streamlining Peer-to-Peer Exchanges..33

4.4 Difficulties and Laws in the DeFi Environment........................ 34

CHAPTER 5...38

Web3 and the Governance Reshaping (DAOs)..........................38

5.1: Decentralized Autonomous Organizations (DAOs): A Novel Approach to Group Decision-Making... 38

5.2 Token-Based Voting and Proposals: DAO Structure and Governance Mechanisms.. 39

5.3 DAOs in Action: From Social Coordination to Investment.......42

5.4 DAOs in the Future: Changing Workplace Collaboration and Decision-Making Procedures... 44

CHAPTER 6...47

Web3 and the Internet's Transformation (dWeb)..................... 47

6.1 Decentralizing the Web (dWeb) to Eradicate Centralized Control. 47

6.2 Distributed Storage Solutions: Safe and Censorship-Resistant Data Storage with Filecoin and IPFS.. 48

6.3 Decentralized Services and Applications: Creating a Web That Is More Accessible and Fair.. 51

6.4 The dWeb and the Prospects for Distribution and Content Creation..53

CHAPTER 7..57
Supply Chain Management and the Revolution with Web3................. 57

7.1 Supply Chains Powered by Blockchain: Guaranteeing Efficiency, Traceability, and Transparency.. 57

7.2 Monitoring Materials and Goods From Origin to Destination in the Supply Chain...58

7.3 Improving Supply Chain Visibility: Up-to-Date Information and Better Teamwork...60

7.4 Web3's Effect on Inventory Management and Logistics................ 62

CHAPTER 8..65
Web3 and the Social Media Restructuring.. 65

8.1 Ownership and Control Returned to Users in Decentralized Social Networks (DSNs)..65

8.2 DSN Monetization: Paying Content Creators and Doing Away with Censorship..67

8.3 Putting Users in Charge of Their Data: Data Privacy and Security in DSNs...68

8.4 The Difficulties and Promise of Distributed Social Media Networks 70

CHAPTER 9..73
Web3 and the Gaming Industry's Reimagining...................................... 73

9.1 Play-to-Earn Gaming: Using Blockchain to Earn Rewards and Own In-Game Assets...73

9.2 Decentralized In-Game Item Marketplaces: Real Ownership and

Compatibility... 75

9.3 Blockchain-Based Games' Ascent: Novel Experiences and Business Models..76

9.4 Web3 and the Democratization of Game Development: The Future of Gaming.. 78

CHAPTER 10..80

The Future Ahead: Web3's Challenges and Opportunities...................80

10.1 Sustainability and Scalability: Handling Difficulties with Blockchain Technology.. 80

10.2 Regulation and Interoperability: Establishing a Structure for Conscientious Innovation..82

10.3 Education and User Adoption: Filling the Divide Between Conventional and Decentralized Systems...85

10.4 The Web3 of the Future: A User-Centric, Fair, and Open Internet... 88

ABOUT THE AUTHOR..92

ACKNOWLEDGMENTS

I sincerely thank everyone who helped to make this book possible.

First and foremost, I want to express my gratitude to my family and friends for their constant support and inspiration along this trip. Your endurance and confidence in me have given me courage and motivation.

Thank you to all of the many practitioners, academics, and professionals in the domains of decentralization and blockchain technology whose groundbreaking work and insights have influenced this book's foundation. I owe a debt of gratitude to the larger Web3 community for its creativity and energy, which never stop pushing the envelope of what's possible.

A particular thank you to the editors and reviewers, whose suggestions and counsel were very helpful in improving the work. Your proficiency and meticulousness have substantially raised the caliber of this work.

Finally, this book was motivated by your curiosity about the revolutionary possibilities of Web3 and decentralized technologies, the readers. As you navigate this dynamic field's future, I hope you find it to be both instructive and inspirational.

I sincerely appreciate all of your wonderful help and efforts.

Disclaimer

This book's content is solely intended for informational and educational purposes. As of the publication date, the content represents the author's comprehension and interpretation of Web3 technologies, blockchain, and decentralized apps.

The author and publisher have taken every precaution to ensure the truth and completeness of the information presented, but they make no guarantees or assurances regarding the content's timeliness, correctness, or dependability. Technology is changing so quickly that new advancements might happen after the article is published, which could change or have an impact on how relevant the material is.

The book should not be regarded as financial, legal, or professional advice because it is not such. Before making decisions based only on the information in this book, readers are advised to see a professional for counsel customized to their particular situation.

The use of or reliance on the information included in this book may result in losses or damages for which the author and publisher shall not be held responsible. Each and every specified trademark, company name, and product name belongs to its rightful owner.

CHAPTER 1

Overview of Decentralization and Web3

1.1 What is Web3?

The next generation of the internet is referred to as Web3.0, or Web3.0, and is defined by decentralized networks and applications that put the needs of users' control, privacy, and ownership first. Web3 seeks to establish a more open, trustless, and permissionless internet than its predecessors, Web1 (a static web) and Web2 (a dynamic and interactive web dominated by centralized platforms).

Key Components of Web3:

- **Decentralized Applications (DApps)** are applications that function without a central authority and are powered by blockchain technology.
- **Smart Contracts:** Automated and trustless transactions made possible by self-executing

contracts that have the terms of the agreement explicitly encoded into code.
- **Cryptocurrencies and Tokens**: Virtual goods that facilitate trade and encourage involvement in decentralized networks.
- **Blockchain:** An immutable, secure, and distributed ledger technology that records transactions.

1.2 Essential Decentralization Concepts

The fundamental idea of Web3 is decentralization, which encourages a move away from centralized control and toward dispersed networks. Numerous facets of technology, governance, and economics are impacted by this idea.

Basic Principles:
- **Distributed Networks:** Instead of being governed by a single body, data and actions are dispersed across several nodes. This promotes increased resilience, lowers the possibility of single points of failure, and improves security.
- **User Empowerment:** Less reliance on centralized

middlemen results from people having more control over their data and digital identities.

- **Transparency and Trust**: Blockchain technology makes sure that all parties can verify transactions and operations, which promotes systemic trust.
- **Permissionless Innovation:** This promotes creativity and inclusivity since anybody can join and contribute to the network without requiring permission from a central authority.

1.3 The Web's Development: From Web1 to Web3

Since its creation, the internet has experienced major modifications, with new capabilities and paradigms emerging at each stage.

Web1: The Static Web
Time period: the 1990s
Features:
- Read-only content
- Static web pages
- Limited interactivity
- Webmasters' centralized management

User Experience: Users had limited ability to create or engage with content, but they could still consume it.

Web2: The Interactive Web

Time period: 2000s to the present

Features:

- Read-write content Dynamic web pages
- High levels of user-generated content and interaction
- Social media platforms' dominance and centralized services

Context of Use: Facebook, Twitter, and YouTube are examples of centralized platforms that allow users to interact, generate content, and engage with others. But these platforms manage data and frequently make money off of user data.

The Decentralized Web, or Web 3.0

Episode: Emerging era

Features:

- Read-write-own content
- Decentralized apps (DApps)
- Integration of smart contracts and blockchain
- Ownership of data and digital assets by users

User Experience: Users can participate in decentralized networks without the need for middlemen and have control over their assets, digital identities, and data.

1.4 The Significance of Decentralization

Decentralization is essential to the Web3 paradigm because it solves the drawbacks and difficulties associated with centralized systems, among other important reasons.

Advantages of Decentralization:
- **Improved Security:** Decentralization reduces the danger of hacking, data breaches, and single points of failure by spreading data and operations across numerous nodes.
- **Better Privacy:** Because users maintain control over their data, there is a lower chance that centralized institutions will gather and use it without authorization.
- Decentralized networks exhibit greater resilience and dependability in the face of disruptions and intrusions, hence guaranteeing uninterrupted availability and dependability.

- **Economic Inclusion:** Especially for the unbanked and underbanked, decentralization democratizes access to financial services and economic opportunity.
- **Transparency and Trust:** By offering an unchangeable and transparent record of transactions, blockchain technology promotes participant trust and eliminates the need for middlemen.

Difficulties and Things to Take Into Account:
- **Scalability:** Making sure decentralized networks can effectively manage high transaction volumes is still a problem.
- **Regulatory Uncertainty:** The adoption of decentralized technology is unpredictable due to the changing regulatory environment.
- **Usability:** Enhancing decentralized applications' usability and accessibility is essential for their broad adoption.
- **Interoperability:** To build a coherent ecosystem, it is imperative to enable smooth communication between various decentralized networks and platforms.

Web3 and decentralization, which prioritize user empowerment, security, and trust, mark a revolutionary change in the architecture of the internet. As technology advances, it has the power to completely transform a number of sectors and our digital lives, opening the door to a more just and accessible internet.

CHAPTER 2

BLOCKCHAIN TECHNOLOGY UNVEILED

2.1 Describe Blockchain. Knowing How to Use the Distributed Ledger System

Blockchain is a cutting-edge technology that establishes a distributed, unchangeable ledger of transactions, providing the foundation for decentralized systems. It guarantees confidence, security, and transparency without the need for middlemen.

Important Features:

- **Distributed Ledger:** A digital document that is synchronized and shared amongst several network nodes (computers). Every node keeps a duplicate of the complete ledger, guaranteeing availability and consistency of data.
- **Blocks and Chains:** Transactions are arranged in groups called blocks, which are connected to one

another in a chain that runs chronologically. To maintain chain integrity, every block has a distinct cryptographic hash of the one before it.
- **Decentralization:** Blockchain functions on a peer-to-peer network, doing away with the necessity for a central authority, in contrast to conventional centralized databases. The decentralized structure improves resilience and security.

How Blockchain Operates:

1. **Transaction Initiation:** A transaction is started by a user and sent out to the network of nodes.
2. **Validation**: To make sure a transaction is valid, network nodes use consensus techniques (such Proof of Work and Proof of Stake).
3. **Block Creation:** After a set of validated transactions is assembled, the block is appended to the blockchain.
4. **Immutable Record:** After a block is added, it becomes an indestructible, publicly viewable, and unchangeable part of the blockchain.

2.2 The Three Fundamental Ideas of Blockchain: Consensus, Transparency, and Immutability

Blockchain technology differs from conventional systems because it is based on a number of core ideas.

Immutability:
- **Clause:** A block cannot be removed or changed once it has been added to the blockchain. The integrity and reliability of the data are guaranteed by their immutability.
- **System:** Based on the contents of each block, the cryptographic hash function generates a unique identity for it. Changes in the block's data would produce a distinct hash, indicating manipulation.

Transparency:
- **Definition:** A blockchain's transactions are fully transparent because they are all viewable to network users.

Advantages:
- **Auditability:** Clear records make transaction

auditing and verification simple.
- **Trust:** Participants' trust is bolstered by easy access to transaction history.

Consensus:
- **Definition:** Consensus mechanisms are protocols that blockchain networks employ to reach consensus regarding the legitimacy of transactions and preserve the ledger's integrity.

Types of Consensus Mechanisms:
- **Proof of Work (PoW):** To validate transactions and produce new blocks, miners compete to find solutions to challenging mathematical puzzles. Significant computational power and energy are needed for this process.
- **Proof of Stake (PoS):** The quantity of coins that validators own and are prepared to "stake" as collateral determines which ones they get to construct new blocks with. PoS uses less energy than PoW does.
- Under **Delegated Proof of Stake (DPoS),** users cast their votes for a select group of delegates who

approve transactions and add new blocks on behalf of the network.

2.3 Distinct Blockchain Types: Permissioned, Private, and Public

Blockchain networks, each with unique features and use cases, can be grouped according to their access and governance frameworks.

Public blockchains are defined as being accessible to everybody who wants to be a part of the network. Anyone can validate and create new blocks, and all transactions are publicly available.

Public Blockchains:
Ethereum and Bitcoin are two examples.

Pros:
- **Decentralization:** High levels of security and decentralization.
- **Transparency:** Complete disclosure of all dealings.

Disadvantages:

- **Scalability:** Limited transaction throughput since several nodes must reach consensus.
- **Energy Consumption:** Significant energy usage, particularly for systems based on PoW.

Private Blockchains:

Hyperledger Fabric and Corda are two examples.

- **Definition:** Exclusive to a particular group or organization. The network is password-protected, and only users with permission can add and validate new blocks.

Advantages:

- **Performance:** Increased efficiency and transaction throughput.
- **Privacy:** Improved transaction secrecy and privacy.

Consequences:

- **Centralization:** Less decentralization since power is held by a single organization or group.
- **Trust:** Trust is dependent upon the body in charge.

Blockchains with Permissions:

As instances: Ripple, Quorum.

- **Definition:** Merge components of public and private blockchains. There are restrictions on access, however several groups can be a part of the network.

Benefits:
- **Managed Access:** Coordinated access with numerous reliable partners.
- **Efficiency:** Harmony between performance and decentralization.

Disadvantages:
- **Complex Governance:** Needs advanced governance mechanisms to control decision-making and access.
- **Partial Decentralization:** A lack of complete decentralization could undermine trust.

2.4 Blockchain Technology's Potential Is Not Limited to Cryptocurrencies

Although blockchain technology is most commonly associated with cryptocurrencies, its applications go much beyond virtual money. Many sectors are investigating blockchain technology in an effort to find novel solutions to challenging issues.

Financial Services:

Use Cases:
- **Cross-Border Payments:** International transactions that are quicker, less expensive, and more transparent.
- **Smart Contracts:** Automated and legally binding agreements for trading stocks, insurance, and loans.

Advantages:

- **Efficiency:** Shorter transaction times and lower expenses.
- **Security:** Improved fraud prevention and security.

Supply Chain Management:

Use Cases:

- **Traceability:** Following the path of commodities from manufacture to delivery.
- **Transparency**: giving customers accurate information about the provenance and legitimacy of products.

Advantages:

- **Responsibility:** Enhanced responsibility and adherence to rules.
- **Efficiency:** Inventory control and logistics were streamlined.

Healthcare:

Use Cases:

- **Medical Records:** Interoperable and secure patient records that authorized providers can access.
- **Drug Traceability:** Monitoring pharmaceutical manufacture and distribution to stop counterfeiting.

Advantages:

- **Data Security:** Improved confidentiality and

protection of private health data.
- **Patient Care:** Better care coordination and standard.

Real Estate:

Use Cases:

- **Property Transactions:** Smart contracts facilitate safe and easy property transfers.
- **Title Management:** Unchangeable, verifiable records of the ownership and history of real estate.
- Reduction in paperwork and processing times is an efficiency.
- **Transparency:** Ownership documents that are easily available.

Public and Government Services:

Use Cases:

- **Voting Systems:** Digital voting platforms that are safe and transparent.
- **Identity Management:** Personal data protection through digital identity solutions.

The advantages include:

Trust:
- Enhanced confidence in governmental institutions and procedures.
- **Efficiency:** decreased administrative expenses and streamlined service delivery.

By improving security, transparency, and efficiency, blockchain technology has the potential to completely alter a variety of industries. It is anticipated that as technology develops more, so will its uses, spurring creativity and opening up new avenues for both individuals and enterprises.

CHAPTER 3

Explaining Decentralized Apps (dApps) in Simple Terms

3.1 Describe dApps. Blockchain-Based Applications

A family of software programs known as decentralized applications, or dApps, operate on a distributed network, usually a blockchain. Blockchain technology is used by dApps, as opposed to traditional apps, which run on centralized servers, to give users a more private, open, and independent experience.

Important dApp Elements:
- **Backend Code**: Functions as a decentralized peer-to-peer network, eliminating the possibility of a single point of failure.
- **Smart Contracts:** Self-executing contracts that enable automated processes without the need for middlemen because the terms of the agreement are directly encoded into the code.

- **Decentralized Storage:** Stores application data securely using distributed storage technologies (like IPFS).
- **User Interface:** Blockchain protocols are used to connect the user interface to the backend and can be constructed using conventional frontend frameworks.

Advantages of decentralized applications (dApps):

- **Security:** Better security because blockchain technology is distributed, which makes it harder for bad actors to compromise the system.
- **Transparency:** Complete traceability and transparency are ensured by the blockchain, which records every operation and transaction.
- **Autonomy**: Once deployed, decentralized applications (dApps) may function independently, eliminating the need for middlemen and centralized management.

3.2 Trustless, Permissionless, and Censorship-Resistant dApp Features

dApps are distinct from conventional centralized apps due to a number of fundamental features.

Trustless:
- **Definition:** To carry out transactions or operations, users do not have to have faith in a centralized authority or middleman.
- **Mechanism:** Without human interference, smart contracts automate and enforce rules, guaranteeing that the conditions are adhered to.

Advantage:

Because all transactions on the blockchain are visible and verifiable, there is less chance of fraud and manipulation.

Permissionless:

Definition: No central authority's permission is required for participation in the network.

Mechanism: Users are free to join and contribute to the network thanks to open protocols and standards.

Advantage:

By permitting unrestricted access to the application, it fosters inclusivity and innovation.

Resistant to Censorship:
- **Definition:** dApps are not susceptible to censorship or dominance by a single party.
- **Mechanism:** Data and processes in decentralized networks are distributed among several nodes, making it more difficult for an entity to censor or change information.

Benefit:
Guarantees that the application will continue to function and be available despite attempts to block or terminate it.

3.3 Popular dApp Examples in Various Industries

dApps are being created and implemented in a number of

industries, showcasing their adaptability and capacity to completely transform established structures.

Finance (DeFi):

- **Uniswap:** A decentralized exchange (DEX) that lets users trade cryptocurrencies independently of a centralized body. It enables automatic liquidity provisioning and trading through the use of smart contracts.
- **Aave:** a decentralized platform for borrowing and lending where users can borrow assets with collateral and receive interest on deposits. It provides safe, clear financial services without the need for middlemen.

Supply Chain Management:

- **VeChain:** A blockchain-based platform that improves the traceability and transparency of the supply chain. Businesses can use it to trace products along the whole supply chain, minimizing fraud and guaranteeing authenticity.

- **Provenance:** A dApp that offers real-time product traceability, enabling customers to confirm the origin and path of items, thus encouraging sustainable and ethical sourcing.

Medical Services:

- **MedRec:** a decentralized electronic health record (EHR) management platform. It guarantees safe and compatible access to patient information, enhancing care coordination and quality.
- **Resolve.Take Care:** a blockchain-based platform for managing healthcare that simplifies procedures including billing, appointment scheduling, and patient-provider collaboration.

Gaming:

- **Axie Infinity**: It is a blockchain-based game in which users gather, breed, and fight Axies, who are fantastical animals. It represents distinct in-game assets that players may trade and possess using NFTs (non-fungible tokens).

- **Decentraland:** Blockchain technology is used to build, explore, and trade digital assets and real estate on this virtual reality platform. It offers a community-run, decentralized virtual environment.

3.4 Developing and Implementing dApps: Resources and Tools

dApp development and deployment require a blend of conventional development resources and technologies tailored to blockchain technology.

Blockchain Platforms:

- **Ethereum:** The most well-liked platform for developing decentralized apps, with a rich developer community, smart contract languages (like Solidity), and a solid ecosystem of developer tools.
- **Binance Smart Chain (BSC):** A blockchain network that attracts dApp developers with its quick and inexpensive transaction speeds.
- **Polkadot:** A multi-chain platform that facilitates communication between many blockchains, enabling

decentralized applications to take advantage of the advantages of several networks.

Development Tools:

- **Truffle Suite:** An Ethereum development environment, asset pipeline, and testing framework that facilitates the creation and implementation of smart contracts.
- **Remix IDE:** An Ethereum blockchain integrated development environment that is web-based and used for creating, evaluating, and implementing smart contracts.
- **Hardhat:** An Ethereum development environment with adaptable tools for creating, evaluating, and implementing smart contracts.

Decentralized Storage Solutions:

- **IPFS (InterPlanetary File System):** A peer-to-peer file sharing and storage system that guarantees secure and decentralized application data storage.
- **Filecoin:** An IPFS-based decentralized storage

network that encourages users to donate store space, resulting in a strong and dispersed storage ecosystem.

Frontend Development:

- **Web3.js:** Frontend Development a JavaScript package that enables developers to communicate with the Ethereum network through their dApps' front ends.
- **Ethers.js:** a small, intuitive library that makes it simple to communicate with the Ethereum network while maintaining security.

Deployment and Testing:

- **Ganache:** An Ethereum development personal blockchain that lets developers conduct tests, deploy contracts, and carry out instructions without requiring a live network.
- **Infura:** An Ethereum and IPFS access service that is scalable and dependable that lets developers connect their dApps to the blockchain without having to

worry about maintaining their own nodes.

Decentralized apps, or dApps, are a big step forward in the software development world. They leverage blockchain technology to improve security, transparency, and user control. dApps have the potential to upend established sectors and provide up new avenues for innovation and expansion as the ecosystem develops.

CHAPTER 4

WEB3 AND FINANCE'S FUTURE (DEFI)

4.1 Decentralized Finance (DeFi): A Financial Services Paradigm Transformation

Using blockchain technology to recreate and enhance established financial systems, Decentralized Finance, or DeFi, is a revolutionary movement in the financial sector. DeFi offers open access to financial services, removes middlemen, and boosts transparency.

Essential Elements of DeFi:

- **Smart Contracts:** Autonomous agreements with conditions encoded directly into the code, allowing for automated financial transactions devoid of middlemen.
- **Decentralized Applications (dApps):** Blockchain-based platforms that provide lending,

borrowing, trading, and insurance are examples of financial services.
- **Tokens and Cryptocurrencies:** Virtual goods that are utilized by DeFi platforms to speed up transactions and encourage involvement.

Advantages of DeFi:

- **Inclusivity:** Gives people without access to traditional banking systems access to financial services.
- **Transparency:** Full visibility and auditability are made possible by the public blockchain, which records every transaction.
- **Security:** Because blockchain technology is decentralized, there is less chance of a single point of failure, providing enhanced security.

4.2 Revolutionizing Conventional Finance: Financing, Debt, and Exchange in DeFi

DeFi's cutting-edge lending, borrowing, and trading solutions are transforming conventional financial services.

Because there are no middlemen involved, these services are more efficient and less expensive.

Lending and Borrowing:

Platforms: Aave, Compound, and MakerDAO are a few examples.

Instrumentation:

- **Lending:** Users can earn interest on their assets by depositing their cryptocurrency holdings into lending pools.
- **Taking Out:** By offering collateral in the form of additional cryptocurrencies, users are able to borrow assets. The maximum amount that can be borrowed is determined by the loan-to-value ratio.

Advantages:

- **Efficiency:** Automated procedures cut down on the time and expenses related to conventional borrowing and lending.
- **Compatibility:** DeFi platforms do not require credit checks or other conventional criteria because they

are available to everyone with an internet connection.

Trading:

Platforms: Uniswap, Sushiswap, and PancakeSwap are a few examples.

Mechanism:
- DeFi trading platforms employ **Automated Market Makers** (AMMs) as a mechanism to provide liquidity. Instead of dealing directly with other dealers, users trade against liquidity pools.
- **Liquidity Providers:** By placing pairs of assets into liquidity pools, users can become liquidity providers and receive fees from trades that take place within the pool.

Advantages:
- Absence of a Central Authority Because there is no central authority involved, there is less chance of censorship and manipulation when trading occurs.
- **Stay Open 24/7:** DeFi platforms are always open, in

contrast to traditional exchanges that have predetermined trading hours.

4.3 DEXs (Decentralized Exchanges): Enabling Users and Streamlining Peer-to-Peer Exchanges

A vital part of the DeFi ecosystem are decentralized exchanges (DEXs), which allow for peer-to-peer cryptocurrency trading without the need for middlemen.

The following are some of the primary characteristics of DEXs:

- **Non-Custodial:** Users maintain control over their money when trading, which lowers the possibility of theft and hacking that come with centralized exchanges.
- **Transparency:** The blockchain records every transaction, making it possible to view an auditable and transparent history of trading.
- **Accessibility:** DEXs facilitate global participation and financial inclusion because they are available to anybody with an internet connection.

Types of DEXs:

1. **Order Book DEXs**: Function like traditional exchanges by keeping an order book containing buy and sell orders. Loopring and dYdX are two examples.
2. **AMM DEXs:** To make transactions easier, use algorithms and liquidity pools. Uniswap, Balancer, and Curve Finance are a few examples.

Advantages of DEXs:

- **Security:** Better security because they are not custodial, which lowers the possibility of fraud and hacking.
- **Censorship Resistance:** Function without a centralized authority, meaning that transactions are difficult to censor or control by a single party.
- **Lower Fees**: Because there are no middlemen, there are lower fees than with traditional exchanges.

4.4 Difficulties and Laws in the DeFi Environment

Although DeFi has many advantages, there are a number of

obstacles and legal issues that must be resolved for the technology to flourish sustainably.

Difficulties:

- **Security Risks:** DeFi is not impervious to security flaws because it is decentralized. Malicious exploits, hacking attacks, and smart contract vulnerabilities can result in large financial losses.
- **Scalability Issues:** A large number of transactions may cause network congestion and higher transaction costs, which may degrade user experience.
- **Context of Use**: DeFi platforms may be complicated and challenging for people who are not familiar with blockchain technology to utilize, which restricts their widespread adoption.

Regulatory Considerations:

- **Compliance:** Adhering to current financial rules and regulations is made more difficult by the absence of established regulatory frameworks for DeFi.
- **AML/KYC Requirements:** Due to DeFi's permissionless architecture, it is challenging to

implement Know Your Customer (KYC) and Anti-Money Laundering (AML) rules, which raises questions about potential criminal activity.
- **Legal Clarity:** Regulators are attempting to ascertain the legal standing of DeFi operations as well as the obligations of platform operators.

Possible Solutions:
- **Security Audits:** Frequent security audits as well as bug bounty programs can assist in locating and resolving DeFi protocol flaws.
- **Layer 2 Solutions:** Roll Ups and side chains are examples of layer 2 scaling solutions that can be implemented to improve scalability and lower transaction costs.
- **User Education:** Raising user awareness of DeFi's hazards and recommended actions can enhance both user safety and overall enjoyment.
- **Regulatory Collaboration:** Creating lucid and encouraging regulatory frameworks in conjunction with regulators can aid in the integration of DeFi into the larger financial system.

Decentralized Finance (DeFi) offers creative ideas that go against established financial structures, marking a dramatic change in the financial environment. DeFi has enormous potential benefits, but for it to expand sustainably and be widely adopted, it will need to address certain issues, including regulatory concerns.

CHAPTER 5

WEB3 AND THE GOVERNANCE RESHAPING (DAOS)

5.1: Decentralized Autonomous Organizations (DAOs): A Novel Approach to Group Decision-Making

Decentralized Autonomous Organizations (DAOs), which use blockchain technology to build open, democratic, and effective organizational structures, are a revolutionary paradigm for governance and group decision-making. DAOs function on a decentralized network, as opposed to traditional organizations, allowing individuals to cooperate and make choices without centralized control.

Essential Elements of DAOs:
- **Smart Contracts**: The foundation of DAOs, smart contracts encapsulate the organization's rules and decision-making procedures, guaranteeing automated and transparent operations.
- **Token Holders:** DAO members possess tokens that

stand for influence and voting power within the group. Holders of tokens are able to suggest and cast votes on initiatives, policies, and reforms.

- **Decentralized Network:** DAOs use a blockchain to distribute power and decision-making among a network of members, which lowers the possibility of corruption and centralized power.

Advantages of DAOs:

- **Transparency:** Complete accountability and visibility are provided by the blockchain's recording of all actions and decisions.
- **Inclusion:** Token holders have the ability to engage in governance, encouraging diversity of thought and inclusivity.
- **Efficiency:** Decision-making is streamlined and administrative overhead is decreased through automated processes.

5.2 Token-Based Voting and Proposals: DAO Structure and Governance Mechanisms

Decentralized decision-making and effective organization

administration are made easier by the form and governance procedures of decentralized autonomous organizations (DAOs). The voting and proposal processes in this procedure are token-based.

Token-depending Voting:

Mechanism:
- **Token Distribution:** Participants receive tokens depending on a number of factors, including investment, initial token offerings, and contributions to the organization.
- **Voting Power:** Token holders have proportionate power over choices as each token normally represents one vote.
- **Voting Procedure:** Within a predetermined time frame, token holders cast their votes on proposals that are presented for review. The blockchain ensures transparency and immutability by recording votes.

Advantages:
- **Participation in Democracy:** Token-based voting

guarantees that every member has a voice in the decisions made by the organization.
- **Security and Transparency:** Blockchain technology ensures that all votes are publicly verifiable and secures the voting process by preventing tampering.

Mechanisms of Proposal:

Mechanism:
- **Submission of Proposals:** Any member may submit a proposal detailing the initiatives or modifications they would want to see carried out for consideration.
- **Review and Discussion:** The community reviews and discusses proposals to provide comments and suggestions for improvement.
- **Selection:** A finalized plan is presented for voting. Smart contracts are used to automatically implement it if the necessary support is obtained.

Advantages:
- **Inclusivity:** Any member may submit ideas and initiatives thanks to the proposal procedure.

- **Performance:** Automated implementation guarantees precise and timely execution of authorized projects.

5.3 DAOs in Action: From Social Coordination to Investment

DAOs are being used in a variety of industries, proving their adaptability and capacity to change conventional organizational structures. Here are a few noteworthy instances:

DAOs for Investments:

The DAO:
- The DAO, one of the first DAOs, was established as a venture capital fund where token owners could make investments in businesses and projects. Even with its initial difficulties, it cleared the path for later investment DAOs.
- **MetaCartel Ventures:** A DAO for investments that provides funding for early-stage projects and applications that are decentralized. Members pool

their resources, make financial decisions as a group, and split the gains and losses.

Social Coordination DAOs:
- **Gitcoin:** An open-source project and developer funding DAO. Gitcoin encourages cooperation and contributions to the open-source environment through grants and rewards.
- **The Genesis DAO of DAOstack:** a decentralized cooperation platform that lets communities establish and run their own DAOs. It promotes social coordination by offering instruments for the production, voting, and governance of proposals.

Service DAOs:
- **dxDAO:** A DAO that oversees and controls the protocols and services related to decentralized finance (DeFi). It gives token owners the power to decide on financing, strategic direction, and protocol updates.
- **MolochDAO:** An Ethereum infrastructure financing DAO. It uses a straightforward governance structure in which participants pool their resources and cast

votes on grant requests to maintain the Ethereum network.

5.4 DAOs in the Future: Changing Workplace Collaboration and Decision-Making Procedures

DAOs have the potential to significantly change how people collaborate and make decisions in a variety of contexts in the future. A number of trends and developments are anticipated as DAOs become more widely understood and as technology advances:

Improved Governance Models:
- **Quadratic Voting:** A voting mechanism that enables users to distribute votes according to the strength of their choices, encouraging more thoughtful deliberation and lessening the sway of major token holders.
- **Liquid Democracy:** A hybrid system that blends representative and direct democracy, enabling voters to assign their votes to others while still having the option to cast direct ballots on significant matters.

Collaboration and Interoperability:

Cross-Chain DAOs:
- DAOs will be able to function across many blockchain networks as interoperability improves, which will increase cooperation and resource sharing.
- **Interactions between DAOs:** DAOs will work together more and more to create networks of autonomous organizations capable of combining resources, exchanging knowledge, and taking on ambitious tasks.

Regulatory and Legal Frameworks:
- Legal Recognition: Initiatives are being made to give DAOs legal standing and frameworks so they can function within the confines of current legal frameworks while preserving their decentralized structure.
- **Norms and Compliance:** Establishing best practices and standards for DAO security, governance, and compliance will assist reduce risks and guarantee long-term growth.

Wider Adoption and Use Cases:

- **Corporate Governance**: Conventional firms can implement DAO principles to enhance decision-making effectiveness, employee involvement, and transparency.
- **Public Sector and Governance:** DAOs can be used by public organizations and governments to promote transparent governance, community involvement, and participatory budgeting.
- **Creative Industries:** DAOs can be used by musicians, artists, and content producers to oversee intellectual property rights, pay royalties, and work together on creative initiatives.

Decentralized Autonomous Organizations, or DAOs, are leading the way in revolutionizing cooperation and governance. DAOs provide transparent, democratic, and effective organizational structures that upend conventional paradigms by utilizing blockchain technology. DAOs have the power to influence how decisions are made and how people work together in a variety of industries as the ecosystem develops.

CHAPTER 6

WEB3 AND THE INTERNET'S TRANSFORMATION (DWEB)

6.1 Decentralizing the Web (dWeb) to Eradicate Centralized Control

The Decentralized Web, or dWeb, is a model of the internet that is more dispersed, transparent, and user-centric than the centralized control model of the past. The Web 2 infrastructure that is now in place mainly relies on centralized servers and services that are managed by a small number of large enterprises. There are a number of issues with this centralization, such as single points of failure, censorship, and data privacy concerns.

- The following are the main tenets of the dWeb: **Decentralization:** Services and data are dispersed throughout a network of nodes, decreasing dependency on centralized servers.
- **Transparency:** Users may confirm how their data is

handled and accessed thanks to open protocols and code.

- **User Empowerment:** By giving users more control over their data and online activities, users may enhance security and privacy.

Advantages of the dWeb:

- **Censorship Resistance:** The data distributed by the dWeb makes it impossible for a single entity to control or censor information because it is spread across numerous nodes.
- **Enhanced Security:** Single points of failure and extensive data breaches are less likely with decentralized systems.
- **Data Ownership:** By maintaining control and ownership over their data, users improve their privacy and sense of confidence in digital services.

6.2 Distributed Storage Solutions: Safe and Censorship-Resistant Data Storage with Filecoin and IPFS

The dWeb depends on distributed storage solutions because

they provide effective, safe, and censorship-resistant data storage. In this field, Filecoin and the InterPlanetary File System (IPFS) are two well-known technologies.

InterPlanetary File System (IPFS):

Mechanism:
- **Content Addressing:** IPFS employs content-addressed data, which means that files are identified not by their server location but by the unique cryptographic hash of their content.
- **Decentralized Network**: Information is kept in a network of nodes, where each node has a subset of the information. IPFS gets a file request from a user and gets it from the closest node with the content.

Advantages:
- **Resistance to Censorship:** Data is difficult to erase or change covertly.
- **Efficiency:** By retrieving files from the closest nodes, latency is decreased and access speeds are increased.
- **Redundancy:** By replicating data among several

nodes, availability is guaranteed even in the event that some nodes fail.

Filecoin:

Mechanism:

- **Incentivized Storage:** Filecoin adds an incentive layer based on blockchain technology to expand upon IPFS. Storage providers receive Filecoin tokens in exchange for providing their storage resources, and users pay for storage space.
- **Storage Proof:** Cryptographic proofs are used by Filecoin to verify that storage providers are storing the data they say they are.

Advantages:

- **Scalability:** By incentivizing storage providers to participate, the incentive model raises the total storage capacity.
- **Security:** Data availability and integrity are guaranteed by cryptographic proofs.
- **Economic Viability:** Users' costs may decrease as a

result of the competitive market for storage services.

6.3 Decentralized Services and Applications: Creating a Web That Is More Accessible and Fair

The core of the dWeb is made up of decentralized applications (dApps) and services that promote an open and equitable internet while offering alternatives to centralized platforms. These apps provide improved security, transparency, and user control by utilizing blockchain and other decentralized technologies.

Important Features of decentralized apps (dApps):

- **Trustless Operations:** Decentralized apps function using smart contracts, which run autonomously according to preset rules, doing away with the need for middlemen.
- **Permissionless Access:** No central authority approval is needed for anyone to use or develop dApps.
- **Censorship Resistance:** The application's decentralized nature makes it challenging for a single party to censor or control it.

Examples of dApps and Services:

- **Decentralized Finance (DeFi):** Without the need for middlemen, platforms like Uniswap, Aave, and Compound provide financial services like lending, borrowing, and trading.
- **Social Media:** Mastodon and Steemit are two alternatives to popular social media sites that allow users more control over the information and interactions they post.
- **markets:** Users can purchase, sell, and trade digital assets with one another directly through decentralized markets like OpenSea and Rarible.

The following are some advantages of dApps:

- **User ownership:** By retaining ownership over their assets and data, users can become less reliant on centralized authorities.
- **Transparency:** The application's operations are transparent and trustworthy thanks to open-source code and blockchain records.
- **Innovation:** The permissionless nature of dApps encourages experimentation and creativity, resulting

in a wide range of original applications.

6.4 The dWeb and the Prospects for Distribution and Content Creation

The distribution and creation of information are about to undergo a radical change thanks to the dWeb, which will solve the drawbacks of centralized platforms and present new avenues for consumers and producers to engage. The dWeb can empower artists, guarantee equitable compensation, and improve content accessibility by utilizing decentralized technologies.

Empowering Creators:
Direct Monetization: Through tokenization, crowdfunding, and microtransactions, decentralized platforms allow creators to directly commercialize their work without the need for middlemen.
Ownership and Control: Content creators are in charge of their work and may dictate how it is distributed and used, which lowers the possibility that centralized platforms will take advantage of them.
Community Engagement: Closer communication

between creators and their audience is made possible by decentralized platforms, which promote a feeling of shared ownership and community.

Improving material Accessibility:
- **Global Reach:** Decentralized networks guarantee that material is reachable from any location, cutting through political and geographic boundaries.
- **Censorship Resistance:** By lowering the possibility of censorship, decentralized content distribution makes it possible for a range of viewpoints to be voiced.
- **Incentivized Distribution:** To ensure content availability and lessen dependency on centralized servers, models such as Filecoin and IPFS provide incentives for content distribution and storage.

Examples of Decentralized Content Platforms:
- **Audius**: is a decentralized music streaming platform that enables musicians to share and profit from their music directly with fans. This is one example of a decentralized content platform.
- **Mirror:** A decentralized publishing platform that

lets authors interact with readers directly by tokenizing their work.
- **Theta:** A decentralized network for video delivery that encourages users to pool their computer power and bandwidth in order to stream videos.

Difficulties and Things to Take Into Account:
- **Usability:** Although decentralized platforms provide many advantages, people who are not familiar with blockchain technology may find them confusing. For adoption to spread, usability and user experience must be improved.
- **Regulation:** Because the dWeb is decentralized, it can be difficult to comply with regulations pertaining to user protection, intellectual property rights, and content control.
- **Scalability:** For the dWeb to succeed in the long run, it is imperative that decentralized networks be able to grow to accommodate the needs of an increasing user population.

The Decentralized Web (dWeb) is a revolutionary idea for how the internet will develop in the future. The dWeb offers an online environment that is more open, safe, and equitable by eschewing centralized authority. The distributed web (dWeb) has the potential to completely change the way we interact with the digital world through new forms of content production and distribution, decentralized apps, and distributed storage solutions. To fully realize Web3's promise, the dWeb will be essential as adoption and technology advance.

CHAPTER 7

SUPPLY CHAIN MANAGEMENT AND THE REVOLUTION WITH WEB3

7.1 Supply Chains Powered by Blockchain: Guaranteeing Efficiency, Traceability, and Transparency

Supply chain management could undergo a transformation thanks to blockchain technology, which offers previously unheard-of levels of efficiency, traceability, and openness. Conventional supply chains frequently include ineffective procedures, fragmented data, and poor visibility. By offering a decentralized, unchangeable ledger where all transactions and data points are recorded and available to authorized participants, blockchain solves these problems.

Major Advantages of Blockchain-Powered Supply Chains:

- **Transparency:** By providing a single, verified

source of truth, all parties involved in the supply chain can access it, which lowers conflict and boosts confidence.
- **Traceability:** The blockchain records each stage of the supply chain, allowing for thorough tracking of products from point of origin to point of destination.
- **Efficiency:** Smart contracts and automated procedures optimize workflows, cutting down on mistakes and delays.

Implementation Examples:
- **Walmart:** Tracks food product origins using blockchain technology, improving food safety by promptly locating contaminated sources.
- **Maersk:** Work with IBM to digitize supply chain documentation using blockchain technology, increasing productivity and cutting expenses associated with administration.

7.2 Monitoring Materials and Goods From Origin to Destination in the Supply Chain

The capacity of blockchain technology to monitor

materials and goods accurately and transparently from their point of origin to their final destination is one of the technology's most important benefits for supply chain management. Ensuring product authenticity, quality control, and regulatory compliance all depend on this end-to-end visibility.

How to Track Goods Using Blockchain:
- **Recording Origin:** Upon creation or harvest, every product is given a digital identity that includes information about its provenance and original state.
- **Transit Monitoring:** At each checkpoint, data from sensors and Internet of Things (IoT) devices, such as location, temperature, and humidity, is added to the blockchain.
- **Verifying Transfers:** The blockchain records each and every exchange of products between parties, giving a comprehensive history of ownership and custody.
- **Confirming Delivery:** The supply chain record is completed when the delivery is verified and recorded upon reaching the final destination.

Advantages:

- **Product Authentication:** By enabling consumers to confirm a product's validity, fraud and counterfeiting are decreased.
- **Quality Assurance:** Constant observation guarantees that products are carried in the best possible ways, preserving quality.
- **Regulatory Compliance:** Open and transparent records make it easier to abide by rules and guidelines in the business.

7.3 Improving Supply Chain Visibility: Up-to-Date Information and Better Teamwork

Modern supply chain management relies heavily on increased visibility, and blockchain technology makes it possible for stakeholders to collaborate better and share data in real time. Better risk management, decision-making, and overall supply chain optimization are made possible by this visibility.

Real-Time Data Sharing:

- **Live Tracking:** Blockchain makes it possible to

trace shipments in real time, giving updates on the whereabouts and state of the items.

- **Data Integration:** The blockchain is combined with data from other sources, such as corporate systems and Internet of Things devices, to provide a comprehensive supply chain picture.

Better Cooperation:

- **Shared Ledger:** Transparency and trust are fostered by granting access to a shared ledger to all supply chain actors.
- **Smart Contracts:** Blockchain-enabled automated contracts simplify transactions and eliminate the need for middlemen.

Use Cases:

- **Provenance:** Businesses are able to track a product's whole lifecycle, guaranteeing sustainable standards and ethical sourcing.
- **Supplier Management:** Better insight into supplier operations enables businesses to recognize and address hazards before they become serious.

7.4 Web3's Effect on Inventory Management and Logistics

Web3 technologies are bringing more efficiency, security, and automation to logistics and inventory management. Examples of these technologies are blockchain and decentralized applications (dApps). These developments save expenses and raise service standards by assisting businesses in managing their supply networks more skillfully.

Logistics:
- **Automated Freight Management:** Blockchain-based systems reduce human error and intervention by automating the management of freight from booking to delivery.
- **Route Optimization:** Smart contracts and real-time data allow for dynamic route optimization, which speeds up deliveries and uses less fuel.
- **Transparent and Secure Transactions**: Decentralized systems guarantee clear and safe financial exchanges between logistics suppliers and customers.

Inventory Management:
- **Accurate Inventory Tracking:** Blockchain reduces inconsistencies and theft by offering a tamper-proof record of inventory levels.
- **Demand Forecasting:** Companies can maintain ideal inventory levels by using real-time data analytics to improve demand forecasting accuracy.
- **Automated restocking:** When stock levels drop below a predetermined threshold, smart contracts have the ability to automatically initiate inventory restocking.

Case Studies:
- **UPS:** Enhances productivity and customer happiness by utilizing blockchain technology to safeguard and optimize logistics procedures.
- **Everledger and IBM:** Work together to trace and identify diamonds, guaranteeing moral sourcing and cutting down on fraud in the supply chain for jewelry.

Future Prospects:
- **Interoperability:** The creation of blockchain networks that are compatible with one another will make it possible for data to be exchanged easily between various platforms and businesses.
- **Artificial Intelligence Integration:** Supply chain optimization, risk management, and predictive analytics can all be improved by combining blockchain technology with AI.

Web3 technologies have the potential to completely transform supply chain management by offering unmatched efficiency, traceability, and transparency. Supply chains enabled by blockchain technology improve communication and visibility while guaranteeing precise tracking of resources and goods from point of origin to point of destination. Web3 has an impact on inventory management and logistics as well, automating procedures and enhancing decision-making. These technologies will be very important in determining how global supply networks develop in the future.

CHAPTER 8

WEB3 AND THE SOCIAL MEDIA RESTRUCTURING

8.1 Ownership and Control Returned to Users in Decentralized Social Networks (DSNs)

Decentralized Social Networks (DSNs) are a paradigm change in social media platforms that provide individual users ownership and control over formerly held by centralized organizations. In traditional social media, a small number of powerful corporations dominate revenue strategies, content filtering, and enormous volumes of user data. DSNs, which are based on blockchain technology, upend this paradigm by giving consumers more control over decentralization.

Important Features of DSNs:
- **User Ownership:** DSNs give users the ability to own their content and data, in contrast to centralized platforms. Every user is in charge of their online

persona and the data they disclose.

- **Decentralized Governance:** DSNs function using models of community-driven governance, frequently including voting mechanisms based on tokens that allow users to suggest and approve platform modifications.
- **Interoperability:** By interacting with other decentralized networks and applications, DSNs make the online experience more integrated and smooth.

Advantages:

- **Enhanced Transparency**: Community votes are used to make clear decisions on platform modifications and content moderation.
- **Decreased Censorship:** A more open exchange of ideas is promoted by a decreased likelihood of content being arbitrarily deleted or censored.
- **Enhanced Privacy:** By giving users more control over the use of their data, users lower the possibility of data abuse.

8.2 DSN Monetization: Paying Content Creators and Doing Away with Censorship

DSNs' monetization strategy, which attempts to directly compensate content creators while lowering dependency on conventional advertising methods, is among its most revolutionary features. This change lessens the necessity for invasive data gathering methods that support censorship and control on centralized platforms while also empowering artists.

DSN Monetization Mechanisms:
- **Token Rewards:** In exchange for their contributions, content creators can receive tokens that can be redeemed on the network or converted for fiat money. Likes, shares, and comments are examples of engagement indicators that are frequently used to distribute tokens.
- **Micropayments:** By allowing users to directly pay authors for small amounts of exclusive material or services, a more enduring and user-driven revenue stream is made possible.
- **Decentralized Advertising:** A few DSNs adopt

decentralized advertising models, in which advertisers have more transparent access to engagement data and users are rewarded for watching ads.

Advantages:
- **Just Remuneration:** Content producers get a more proportionate cut of the money made by their work.
- **Decreased Dependency on Ads:** DSNs can lessen the impact of advertisers and the requirement for data-driven targeting by varying their sources of income.
- **Empowerment:** By giving users and creators greater influence over their online experiences, this promotes a more robust digital ecosystem.

8.3 Putting Users in Charge of Their Data: Data Privacy and Security in DSNs

DSNs prioritize data security and privacy because they seek to address the many problems related to data exploitation on centralized platforms. DSNs give users strong controls over how their data is handled and protected by utilizing blockchain and cryptography technology.

Important Characteristics for Data Security and Privacy:
- **Decentralized Data Storage:** By storing data across a network of nodes as opposed to centralized servers, the possibility of significant data breaches is decreased.
- **End-to-End Encryption:** Data transfers and communications are encrypted to make sure that only the intended parties may access the data.
- **User Consent:** Usually through the use of granular permission settings, users have explicit control over what data is shared and with whom.

Advantages:
- **Improved Security:** Large-scale data breaches are more difficult for hackers to accomplish thanks to decentralized architecture.
- **Better Privacy:** Users keep ownership of their personal data, reducing the possibility of abuse.
- **Transparency:** Users can understand how their

information is managed since data handling procedures are transparent.

8.4 The Difficulties and Promise of Distributed Social Media Networks

Although DSNs have many benefits, there are a number of issues that must be resolved before they can reach their full potential. As the world of decentralized social media changes, developers, consumers, and legislators must comprehend these difficulties.

Challenges:
- **Scalability:** Because decentralized networks can be slower and less effective than their centralized equivalents, scalability problems are a common problem for DSNs.
- **User Adoption:** It takes a lot of work and creativity to draw and keep users in an industry where well-established platforms predominate.
- **Regulatory Obstacles:** For decentralized systems, navigating the various regulations across many jurisdictions can be challenging.

- **User Experience:** Because of the complexity of the underlying technology, ensuring a smooth and simple user experience on DSNs is difficult yet essential for widespread adoption.

Potential:
- **Empowerment:** DSNs can promote a more fair and empowering digital environment by granting users control over their data and content.
- **Innovation:** Since decentralized DSNs don't have centralized gatekeepers, developers are free to develop new features and services.
- **Resilience:** Decentralized networks are more resistant to censorship and outages by nature, which encourages a more open and liberated internet.
- **Growth Driven by the Community:** DSNs can change over time to better meet the needs and interests of their users as a result of community involvement and growth.

By placing a premium on user ownership, privacy, and fair monetization, Web3 and decentralized social networks have the ability to drastically change the social media landscape. Although there are still obstacles to overcome, the further advancement and uptake of DSNs offer a digital environment that is more user-focused, safe, and transparent. It will be crucial to solve these issues and realize the full potential of decentralized social media platforms as technology advances.

CHAPTER 9

WEB3 AND THE GAMING INDUSTRY'S REIMAGINING

9.1 Play-to-Earn Gaming: Using Blockchain to Earn Rewards and Own In-Game Assets

Play-to-earn (P2E) gaming, which uses blockchain technology to open up new business prospects for gamers, is a revolutionary development in the gaming sector. Conventional gaming models tend to favor publishers and developers over players, frequently depriving them of any financial compensation for their labor and time invested in the game. With P2E games, on the other hand, users can actually acquire their in-game belongings and receive prizes.

The following are the main elements of P2E gaming:
- **Blockchain Integration:** Transparency and security are ensured by the blockchain recording of in-game money and assets.

- **Non-Fungible Tokens (NFTs):** Exclusive in-game goods are denoted by NFTs, which let users purchase, exchange, and sell them apart from the actual game.
- **Token Rewards:** In exchange for their accomplishments and engagement, players receive cryptocurrency tokens, which can be traded for real money.

Advantages:
- **Economic Incentives:** Games allow players to earn money, making them a viable form of employment.
- **Asset Ownership:** Having true ownership over in-game assets enables users to exchange goods with one another and create a secondary market outside of the game.
- **Engagement:** By offering material rewards for time and effort expended, P2E models improve player engagement.

9.2 Decentralized In-Game Item Marketplaces: Real Ownership and Compatibility

True ownership and cross-platform compatibility of in-game items are made possible by decentralized marketplaces. Decentralized markets use blockchain technology to enable unrestricted trade and interoperability of digital assets, in contrast to typical centralized game economies where goods are locked within a certain game and controlled by the makers.

The following are the main features:
- **Ownership:** Since in-game assets are kept on the blockchain as NFTs, players have total ownership over them.
- **Interoperability:** The ability to utilize items in many games and platforms increases their usefulness and worth.
- **Transparency:** By guaranteeing clear ownership records and transactions, blockchain technology lowers the possibility of fraud.

Advantages:

- **Liquidity:** Because players are free to purchase, sell, and trade their assets, the market for in-game goods is lively and liquid.
- **Value Retention**: In-game things have value even after they are no longer in the game, giving players long-term advantages.
- **Innovation:** To promote innovation and cooperation in the industry, developers are urged to make compatible games.

9.3 Blockchain-Based Games' Ascent: Novel Experiences and Business Models

A new gaming genre called blockchain-based games is starting to take off, offering distinctive gameplay and cutting-edge business concepts. These games use novel elements including player-driven economy, decentralized governance, and improved security through the use of blockchain technology.

Important Features:

- **Decentralized Economies:** Through their choices

and actions, players directly affect the in-game economy.

- **Governance:** Decentralized autonomous organizations (DAOs) are a common feature in blockchain games that let players take part in decision-making and governance.
- **Security:** Blockchain technology offers strong security features that guard against hackers and cheating while maintaining the integrity of the game.

Advantages:

- **Involvement:** Governance models and economies powered by players boost participation and money in the virtual world.
- **Innovation:** By integrating cutting-edge mechanisms and experiences, blockchain-based games challenge the conventions of traditional game design.
- **Economic Opportunities:** By generating real-world value from their in-game actions, players can develop new gaming-related economic models.

9.4 Web3 and the Democratization of Game Development: The Future of Gaming

The development of video games is about to become more accessible and collaborative thanks to Web3 technologies. Developers may produce and distribute games more effectively by utilizing decentralized platforms and tools, and players and creators can participate in and profit from the game's success.

Important Trends:
- **Decentralized Development Platforms:** Users can produce and profit from their own gaming experiences and content by using platforms like Decentraland and The Sandbox.
- **Crowdfunding and Community Support:** Independent developers can raise money for and work on their projects thanks to blockchain-based models for community support and crowdfunding.
- **Collaborative creation:** Innovation and community-driven game creation are made possible by decentralized governance and collaborative technologies.

Advantages:
- **Accessibility:** A greater variety of creators can now pursue game production due to lower entry barriers.
- **Innovation:** Creative thinking and innovation are encouraged via community-driven creation, which produces a wider variety of original games.
- **Economic Empowerment:** By retaining greater control and making more money from their work, developers and creators can become less dependent on traditional publishers.

Play-to-earn models, decentralized markets, and blockchain-based games are some of the ways that Web3 technologies are revolutionizing the gaming sector. These developments offer players new financial prospects, real in-game asset ownership and interoperability, and easier access to cooperative game production. Web3 will be crucial in influencing how gaming develops going forward, helping to make it more inventive, fair, and enjoyable for all players.

CHAPTER 10

The Future Ahead: Web3's Challenges and Opportunities

10.1 Sustainability and Scalability: Handling Difficulties with Blockchain Technology

Scalability:
Scalability and sustainability are still major issues for Web3 technologies that must be resolved for them to be widely used and function well.

- The capacity of a blockchain network to manage a growing volume of users and transactions without sacrificing efficiency is known as scalability.
- **Current Limitations:** During times of strong demand, many current blockchain networks experience scaling problems, such as poor transaction speeds and excessive fees.

Under Development Solutions:
- **Layer 2 Solutions:** By operating on top of the primary blockchain, technologies like state channels and side chains can lower costs and boost transaction throughput.
- **Sharding:** a technique that splits the blockchain into more manageable chunks (shards), each capable of taking on a certain percentage of network transactions.
- **Innovations in Consensus Mechanisms**: New consensus algorithms that strive to increase scalability without sacrificing security, include Proof of Stake (PoS) and Proof of Authority (PoA).

Sustainability:
- The concept of sustainability in blockchain technology pertains to reducing the environmental impact of blockchain activities, namely the energy consumption resulting from consensus procedures.
- **Present Problems:** Proof of Work (PoW) consensus procedures, which are energy-intensive and have a substantial carbon footprint, are employed by networks such as Bitcoin.

The following are sustainable alternatives:
- **Proof of Stake (PoS):** An energy-efficient consensus process that lessens the requirement for mining operations that require a lot of resources.
- The implementation of energy-efficient technologies and renewable energy sources using blockchain networks is one of the **green initiatives.**

Advantages of Tackling Sustainability and Scalability:
- **Enhanced Efficiency:** Enhanced scalability results in quicker transactions and lower expenses, which makes blockchain technology more useful for daily use.
- **Environmental Impact:** Sustainable operations lower blockchain's carbon footprint, supporting more general environmental objectives.

10.2 Regulation and Interoperability: Establishing a Structure for Conscientious Innovation

As Web3 technologies advance, creating a legal framework and guaranteeing compatibility are essential to encouraging responsible innovation and guaranteeing a smooth user experience.

Regulation:
- **Importance:** Regulatory frameworks offer rules and recommendations to guarantee the moral and secure application of Web3 technologies, safeguarding consumers and advancing market integrity.

The present regulatory landscape is fragmented due to the following reasons:

Differing Regulations:
- Cryptocurrencies, smart contracts, and decentralized finance (DeFi) are governed by different laws in different nations.
- **Compliance:** It might be challenging to make Web3 projects abide by current laws, such as those pertaining to know-your-customer (KYC) and anti-money laundering (AML).

Achievable Methods:
- **Global Cooperation:** Working together, governments and regulatory agencies can develop

standardized frameworks and standards for Web3 technology.
- **Industry Self-Regulation:** To proactively address regulatory challenges, the Web3 community has developed best practices and self-regulatory standards.

Interoperability:

- **Definition:** Interoperability is the capacity of various blockchain networks and decentralized apps (dApps) to cooperate and exchange data in an easy-to-understand manner.

Current Issues:

- **Fragmentation:** Varying blockchain networks' incompatibilities and lack of standards might impede functionality and impede user experience.
- **Integration Challenges:** Cross-platform and cross-technology integration can be resource- and technically-intensive.

Under Development:

- **Cross-Chain Protocols:** Innovations like Polkadot

and Cosmos that provide communication and interaction between various blockchain networks.
- **Standardization:** Initiatives to establish widely accepted guidelines and procedures for blockchain compatibility.

The following are the advantages of addressing regulation and interoperability:
- **Enhanced Security:** Regulatory frameworks assist in risk mitigation and shield users from fraud and security breaches.
- **Fast and Easy User Interface**: The whole Web3 experience is improved by improved interoperability, which enables users to interact with various platforms and services easily.

10.3 Education and User Adoption: Filling the Divide Between Conventional and Decentralized Systems

By addressing user acceptance and education, Web3 technologies must close the gap between traditional systems and decentralized platforms in order to be widely used.

User Adoption:

Current barriers:

- **Complexity:** Web3 technologies sometimes include intricate concepts and user interfaces that can be daunting to novice users.
- **Restricted Use Cases**: In contrast to well-established conventional systems, Web3 technologies may have fewer real-world applications.

Adoption strategies

- User-friendly interfaces aim to streamline the user experience through the creation of easily navigable and easily accessible interfaces.
- **Incentives:** Giving users incentives to test Web3 applications, including prizes or lowered costs.
- **Collaborations:** Joint ventures with popular businesses and platforms to incorporate Web3 functionalities and expand the target market.

Education:
- **Importance:** In order to promote adoption and understanding, users must be educated about Web3 technologies, their advantages, and successful usage techniques.

Existing Difficulties:
- **Inadequate Materials and Resources**: Users desiring to learn about Web3 technologies have limited access to instructional materials and resources.
- **Myths:** There are enduring falsehoods and misconceptions regarding blockchain technology and decentralized systems that must be dispelled.

Educational Initiatives:
- **Workshops and Webinars:** Planning online courses and educational events to give people practical experience and advice.
- **Community Engagement:** Supplying information and responding to queries through community-driven platforms and forums.

Advantages of Focusing on User Education and Adoption:
- **More Participation:** More users will be eager to interact with Web3 technologies, spurring development and expansion within the ecosystem.
- **Informed Decisions:** Users with greater knowledge can choose to use Web3 platforms in more safe and efficient ways by making better-informed decisions.

10.4 The Web3 of the Future: A User-Centric, Fair, and Open Internet

Web3 aims to change how people engage with technology and with one another by creating a more user-centric, egalitarian, and open internet.

The term "open internet" refers to the unfettered and free access to information and services that promotes creativity and innovation.

Principal Patterns:
- A focus on decentralized networks and systems that lessen need on centralized authorities is known as

decentralization.
- **Open Source**: Supporting open-source development methodologies that foster cooperation and openness.

The egalitarian internet guarantees that all users, irrespective of their location or background, have equal access to opportunities and resources.

Prime Trends:

- **Technology Access:** Initiatives to increase underprivileged areas' and communities' access to Web3 technologies.
- The creation of platforms and apps that are inclusive and accessible to all users is known as **inclusive design.**

The concept of a user-centric internet is as follows: it gives users more control and autonomy over their online experiences by prioritizing their needs and preferences.

Principal Patterns:

- Increased emphasis on user privacy and data security, with users having more authority over their

personal data.
- **Customization:** Possibilities for users to personalize their online interactions and use technology in ways that best fit their tastes.

The Future Web3 Vision offers the following advantages:
- **Empowerment:** By giving users more control over their digital life, users become more autonomous and empowered.
- **Innovation:** A creative and open internet promotes innovation, which propels new business ventures and technical developments.
- **cooperation:** Using a user-centric approach promotes community-driven development and cooperation, which improves the Web3 experience as a whole.

Conclusively, Web3 technologies present immense potential for transforming the internet; nonetheless, it is imperative to tackle obstacles associated with scalability, sustainability, regulation, interoperability, user adoption, and education. Web3 can lead the way towards a digital future that is more user-centric, egalitarian, and open by seizing these opportunities and conquering the related obstacles.

ABOUT THE AUTHOR

Author and thought leader in the IT field Taylor Royce is well known. He has a two-decade career and is an expert at tech trend analysis and forecasting, which enables a wide audience to understand complicated concepts.

Royce's considerable involvement in the IT industry stemmed from his passion with technology, which he developed during his computer science studies. He has extensive knowledge of the industry because of his experience in both software development and strategic consulting.

Known for his research and lucidity, he has written multiple best-selling books and contributed to esteemed tech periodicals. Translations of Royce's books throughout the world demonstrate his impact.

Royce is a well-known authority on emerging technologies and their effects on society, frequently requested as a speaker at international conferences and as a guest on tech podcasts. He promotes the development of ethical technology, emphasizing problems like data privacy and the digital divide.

In addition, with a focus on sustainable industry growth, Royce mentors upcoming tech experts and supports IT education projects. Taylor Royce is well known for his ability to combine analytical thinking with technical know-how. He sees a time when technology will ethically benefit humanity.

www.ingramcontent.com/pod-product-compliance
Lightning Source LLC
Chambersburg PA
CBHW071940210526
45479CB00002B/755